CONGRATULATIONS TO MANCHESTER CITY FC
2013/14 BARCLAYS PREMIER LEAGUE CHAMPIONS

Luckily, we provide a generous baggage allowance on all our flights.

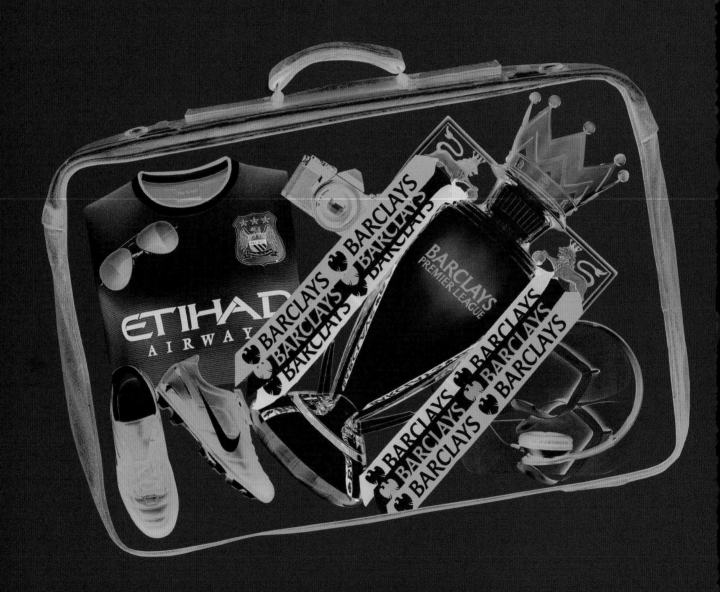

Etihad Airways. Proud partner
of Manchester City FC.

MANCHESTER CITY
FOOTBALL CLUB

#CHAMPIONS 2013/14

Content: David Clayton. **Photos:** MCFC offical photographer Sharon Latham, PA Pics.
Produced by Trinity Mirror Sport Media. **Managing Director:** Ken Rogers. **Publishing Director:** Steve Hanrahan. **Executive Art Editor:** Rick Cooke.
Senior Editor: Paul Dove. **Production:** Roy Gilfoyle **Writer:** Chris Brereton. **Sub-editor:** Alan Jewell. **Design:** Colin Harrison, James Cleary, Mark Frances, Adam Ward

BLUE BEAUTY!

It may not have been as jaw-droppingly dramatic as two years ago, but the Etihad Stadium was the scene of another joyous celebration as we sealed our second Barclays Premier League title in three seasons.

Players, staff and supporters came together as the pitch was engulfed by a sea of blue on the final whistle, following a 2-0 victory over West Ham United that confirmed we would be crowned champions once again.

Goals from Samir Nasri and our inspirational skipper, Vincent Kompany, ensured a relatively stress-free coronation.

It was a title achieved in brilliant fashion overall, with 102 glorious goals across the 38 games, from a team that possesses style and substance.

The blue moon continues to rise...

MANCHESTER CITY 2
WEST HAM UNITED 0
Etihad Stadium, 11.05.14

Another May afternoon at the Etihad Stadium, another date with destiny.

When Sergio Aguero breathtakingly ended City's 44-year wait for a top-flight title two seasons ago thanks to his late, late, strike against QPR, many Blues fans thought they had witnessed the club's finest hour.

In one sense they had; few adrenaline rushes will ever match the moment Aguero hit the back of the net.

However, the victory over West Ham United on Sunday, May, 11, 2014 should be remembered with equal prominence and pride.

It was just as glorious an occasion and perhaps one of even more important and long-lasting significance because if Aguero had secured City's place on English football's top table, the Hammers victory emphatically confirmed it.

A goal in each half from Samir Nasri and Vincent Kompany was enough to see off the Hammers and ensure Liverpool's win over Newcastle United counted for nothing.

It's the first time City have won two trophies in one season >>

>> since 1970, with Manuel Pellegrini's side timing their sprint to the finish line perfectly following five successive victories.

This was not a day for the faint-hearted. On paper and current form, City at home to West Ham looked a fairly straightforward game for the Blues, but with Liverpool waiting in the wings for any slip-ups and the sheer unpredictability of the Premier League in mind, no home supporter was taking anything for granted.

Manuel Pellegrini made just one change from the team that gradually wore down a stubborn Aston Villa resistance in midweek with the return of Aguero and James Milner dropped to the bench as a result.

The Blues were welcomed onto the pitch with a spine-tingling rendition of Blue Moon and once the hand-shakes and formalities were complete, the stage was finally set for the latest chapter in this wonderful club's history.

From the opening few minutes it became clear that the visitors' game plan was containment with often 10 men behind the ball as City probed for a way through the West Ham wall and save for a David Silva volley and an Aleks Kolarov howitzer that Adriano did well to tip over, it looked as though the first half would end goalless.

Indeed, the loudest cheer had been saved for the news that Liverpool had fallen behind on 20 minutes, but finally, just before the break, the Etihad Stadium erupted as Nasri, tired of trying to play his way through the wall of Irons, hit a powerful drive from 20 yards that brushed Adrian's fingers on its way into the net.

With just five minutes to go before the break, it was perfect timing from the Frenchman and settled any lingering nerves on the pitch and in the stands.

If that goal had given the Blues a deserved lead, within four minutes of the re-start, it seemed as though the hosts' advantage was unassailable as - fittingly - captain Kompany popped up to prod the ball home and make it 2-0 from close range.

City had chances to add to their total as the game wore on, but the defence was solid throughout and Joe Hart was a virtual spectator from start to finish.

When the final whistle was blown, the pitch quickly disappeared as thousands of fans poured on to the pitch to celebrate the triumph and one of the greatest Premier League seasons was finally over.

Belief was the key - the players, manager and supporters never stopped believing that City would eventually climb into pole position and like a thoroughbred horse cutting through the field, as others faltered in the final furlong, the Blues hit the front and crossed the finish line first. The mark of true champions.

MANCHESTER CITY: J Hart, M Demichelis, V Kompany, P Zabaleta, A Kolarov, Y Toure (A Negredo, 86), Javi Garcia, D Silva (J Milner, 76), S Nasri, S Aguero, E Dzeko (Fernandinho, 69). Unused: Lescott, Clichy, Pantilimon, Jovetic.

WEST HAM UNITED: Adrian, J O'Brien, W Reid, J Tomkins, G McCartney, S Downing, M Noble, M Diame (J Cole, 81), M Taylor, K Nolan (M Jarvis, 64), A Carroll (C Cole, 72). Unused: Armero, Vaz Te, Collins, Jaaskelainen.

GOALS: Nasri 29, Kompany 49

REFEREE: Martin Atkinson

ATTENDANCE: 47,300

FINAL 2013/14 PREMIER LEAGUE TABLE

	Team	Pld	W	D	L	F	A	GD	Pts
1	**Man City**	38	27	5	6	102	37	65	86
2	Liverpool	38	26	6	6	101	50	51	84
3	Chelsea	38	25	7	6	71	27	44	82
4	Arsenal	38	24	7	7	68	41	27	79
5	Everton	38	21	9	8	61	39	22	72
6	Tottenham	38	21	6	11	55	51	4	69
7	Man United	38	19	7	12	64	43	21	64
8	Southampton	38	15	11	12	54	46	8	56
9	Stoke City	38	13	11	14	45	52	-7	50
10	Newcastle	38	15	4	19	43	59	-16	49
11	Crystal Palace	38	13	6	19	33	48	-15	45
12	Swansea City	38	11	9	18	54	54	0	42
13	West Ham	38	11	7	20	40	51	-11	40
14	Sunderland	38	10	8	20	41	60	-19	38
15	Aston Villa	38	10	8	20	39	61	-22	38
16	Hull City	38	10	7	21	38	53	-15	37
17	West Brom	38	7	15	16	43	59	-16	36
18	Norwich City	38	8	9	21	28	62	-34	33
19	Fulham	38	9	5	24	40	85	-45	32
20	Cardiff City	38	7	9	22	32	74	-42	30

CHAMPIONS
REACTION

"I JUST THINK THAT IF WE KEEP THE SAME SQUAD AND ADD ONE OR TWO GOOD PLAYERS, I DON'T SEE WHY WE CAN'T REPEAT THIS KIND OF THING."

SAMIR NASRI

"I'm really happy, it was really good. We did the job and we knew a draw was enough but that's not the way we play. It's been a fantastic season and we finish with two trophies. We came to win. We play attractive, offensive football. What happened two years ago was important for us because we have matured. It has been fantastic because we have two trophies and it is my second title in three years. I'm really happy and I want to thank the manager.

"The best team won the league in the end. We scored 102 goals in the league, over 150 goals in all competitions, and we always play - a draw would have been enough, but this is the way we play football.

"I just think that if we keep the same squad and add one or two good players, I don't see why we can't repeat this kind of thing."

"I MANAGE A GREAT GROUP OF PLAYERS, A GREAT INSTITUTION AND GREAT FANS. I MUST BE CALM DURING THE GAME TO TAKE DECISIONS BUT WHEN YOU ACHIEVE THE TITLE..."

MANUEL PELLEGRINI

"It's not just winning titles that is important, but it's the way you win them. Big teams cannot be satisfied with one title. It's very important. Celebrate today and Monday, and on Tuesday start working for next season because this club and players deserve more titles.

"The most important thing was we changed the way this team played. I like to play another way and it was very important to give the reasons and have the trust of the players. Maybe if we didn't win the title it would be a very good reason because it was my first season but I did not want to give an excuse. I think it was a season that all of us enjoy, the fans, the players, me also because they see the way we play.

"I manage a great group of players, a great institution and great fans. I must be calm during the game to take decisions but when you achieve the title...

"The fans enjoyed the whole season - we broke the records for the most goals scored by any team in England. It is the way we must play with the quality of players we have.

"Of course I am proud to manage this group of players and this club. It's a great honour to be the first manager from outside of Europe to win the title but I'm not the most important person."

"I AM SO HAPPY, I AM SO GLAD TO HELP MY TEAM, AND I AM SO PROUD TO PLAY FOR THIS TEAM. I THINK I MADE THE RIGHT DECISION TO COME TO ENGLAND AND MAN CITY."

FERNANDINHO

"Today was amazing, by the fans, the club, the team - everyone was concentrated to get the result. In that moment you don't know exactly what you say because the emotion is so high. To win the Premier League is amazing, and in the first season it is doubly amazing.

"I am so happy, I am so glad to help my team, and I am so proud to play for this team. I think I made the right decision to come to England and Man City. I always say in football and life you have to win the title, and Man City gave me the chance to win the title. I am so happy for that.

"The players deserved it. We worked very hard and today was the best way to win the title. In the game we played very good football and we deserved that."

VINCENT KOMPANY

"We're building a club, not just a team. That's why I'm excited to be here, that's why every single year I have a feeling we need to be better, and next year we need to be even better.

"If we want to be a big club, this should be one of so many. It will take a lot of work, but people are ready for it.

"It's unbelievable. I think this team has got more than just talent, it's got a real soul and a heart to it and I'm incredibly happy for this team.

"I'm prepared for anything in football. Whenever we do well I'm happy for this club and the fans.

"The way we have finished this season is a credit to how we have always prepared, every single game and how we have always believed in ourselves. To see the fans and how happy they are, it's just unbelievable."

"IT'S UNBELIEVABLE. I THINK THIS TEAM HAS GOT MORE THAN JUST TALENT, IT'S GOT REAL SOUL AND A HEART TO IT AND I'M INCREDIBLY HAPPY FOR THIS TEAM."

PABLO ZABALETA

"Everyone is trying to work to make this club even bigger.

"It's another trophy. We know how special the Premier League is. To finish like this, it's just fantastic.

"It is amazing. We need to be proud. We know the owners have been spending big over the last few years and now it is happened. We need to enjoy it.

"We are hungry for more. We need to work for more."

"IT'S ANOTHER TROPHY. WE KNOW HOW SPECIAL THE PREMIER LEAGUE IS. TO FINISH LIKE THIS, IT'S JUST FANTASTIC."

DAVID SILVA

"I'm so happy now. The fans have supported us throughout the season like they always do and I'm happy for the whole squad. It's been a long and tough year but in the end we've won two titles so I'm very happy. It's been very difficult. There have been many teams fighting but in the end, we've won so it's even more satisfying. There have been many difficult moments but we have overcome and in the end we deserve this league.

"We've played attacking football and that has helped us score many goals. We like having the possession and playing an attractive style for our supporters.

"I'm fortunate to have won everything and now my second Premier League title. But football never stops so next year we will be back even stronger.

"We're champions but it's not about coming here for money and all these stories we've heard. We've dreamed of this moment all of our lives, when we were kids, when we had no money, when we had nothing. Now we are the champions and that's all it's about. You see the fans and how happy they are. It's just unbelievable."

"I'M FORTUNATE TO HAVE WON EVERYTHING AND NOW MY SECOND PREMIER LEAGUE TITLE. BUT FOOTBALL NEVER STOPS SO NEXT YEAR WE WILL BE BACK EVEN STRONGER."

"THIS IS THE SECOND TITLE IN THREE YEARS AND THAT'S AN AMAZING ACHIEVEMENT FOR US. I'M JUST HAPPY AND PROUD TO BE PART OF THIS TEAM AND THIS CLUB AND I'M HAPPY TO HELP."

SERGIO AGUERO

"I'M VERY HAPPY. I WILL COME BACK STRONGER NEXT YEAR TO WIN MORE TROPHIES."

YAYA TOURE

"I'm very proud and happy this was an amazing season. The club and the fans and the people who work at the club deserve this trophy. I think the team was unbelievable this season. Liverpool gave us a really, really good challenge. We are looking forward to next year now because we are always looking at the future and we want to do better next year."

"I'M VERY PROUD AND HAPPY THIS WAS AN AMAZING SEASON. THE CLUB AND THE FANS AND THE PEOPLE WHO WORK AT THE CLUB DESERVE THIS TROPHY."

"IT'S SOMETHING WE CAN BE REALLY PROUD OF. I'M REALLY PROUD OF OUR GOALKEEPERS AS A WHOLE. WE'RE HAPPY FOR EVERYONE."

"TO COME THROUGH AND WIN SHOWS THE CHARACTER OF THIS SQUAD. YOU HAVE TO ENJOY IT WHILE IT COMES BECAUSE YOU CONCENTRATE ON RETAINING IT."

THE ENGINEER

UNFLAPPABLE PELLEGRINI HAS CHARMED US ALL

In Chile they call him 'The Engineer' and after just one season, City fans know exactly why after Manuel Pellegrini engineered a Capital One Cup victory and the Premier League title in his first year in English football.

The City fans have created a flag in his honour that simply says 'This Charming Man' – and his integrity, calmness and gentle approach has made him a huge favourite with the Blues' followers.

The man from Santiago made his name as an attack-minded coach during his years at Villarreal, Real Madrid and Malaga and when Roberto Mancini left the club last year, Pellegrini was identified as the man who could take the Blues to the next level.

From day one when City dismantled

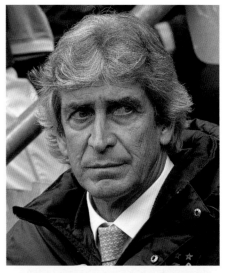

Newcastle 4-0 at the Etihad Stadium, the football Pellegrini's City have played has thrilled and entertained in equal measure with goals coming by the bucket-load and often, the football was sublime.

There were hiccups along the way and just four points from a possible 18 from the first six games on the road perhaps stopped City from picking up the baton and opening a healthy lead at the top, but Pellegrini and his side recovered to end the season as one of the Premier League's most potent away sides.

Pellegrini insisted that the league is decided in May, not at Christmas and continually kept a lid on expectations.

>>

Manuel loved: He may be understated but it doesn't mean the fans don't adore him

>> He set the tone at his unveiling, declaring that "I'm not concerned about finishing second. I'm not concerned about the pressures", and that nerveless, meticulous approach has stood us in good stead ever since.

When the vultures were hovering in the early days of the campaign and questions were being asked of whether Pellegrini could lead the Blues to the title, he remained calm and collected throughout, always believing in his players and continuing to play attacking football.

A few months later, when City again went goal crazy, scoring five against Tottenham Hotspur - the eighth time that figure had been reached in a season that had not yet reached February - Pellegrini was again at his tranquil best.

"I don't even want to talk about the title at the moment," he said. "There is still no silverware, a lot of games are to be played. We'll stay calm and prepare for the next game."

As Arsenal, Liverpool and Chelsea swapped positions at the top of the table, the Blues lurked behind, chasing glory on four fronts and eventually winning the first domestic trophy of the season with a Capital One Cup triumph over Sunderland.

The games in hand meant that the table wasn't quite what it seemed and Pellegrini was always confident his players would deliver and on the final day, they did exactly that, beating West Ham to clinch the title.

A man with great dignity, a man who wants to entertain - Manuel Pellegrini has already delivered two trophies in his first City season and he has done it with style.

This Charming Man indeed...

SIX
STEPS TO THE TITLE
THE BIGGEST MOMENTS OF THE SEASON

MANCHESTER CITY 4
MANCHESTER UNITED 1
22.09.13

PERFECT DERBY DOUBLE

Beating our oldest, and nearest, rivals is always the sweetest of feelings but our ability to defeat the now deposed Barclays Premier League champions so heavily on two occasions underlined City's determination to wrestle the title back from the red half of Manchester.

The first contest in September was Manuel Pellegrini and David Moyes's first Manchester derby as respective managers and the Blues boss was by far the happier individual as we routed United with ease.

Sergio Aguero and Yaya Toure – in a further sign of what was to come – showed their class as they put us 2-0 up at half-time before a further Aguero goal and a strike from Samir Nasri ensured that bragging rights in the Etihad and beyond went well and truly with the home fans.

Wayne Rooney scored a free-kick late on but that was merely a consolation for the stunned visitors.

City were in the ascendancy from the start and Aguero's 16th-minute volley was a reward for their early efforts. We had to wait until first-half injury time to double the lead as Toure got the final touch following a Nasri corner but after the break, Aguero made it 3-0 almost immediately as he side-footed home before Nasri then twisted the knife even further as he volleyed past David De Gea.

That sent the home fans wild and although Rooney tried to make the scoreline more respectable, City's title ambitions were well and truly up and running.

In the away fixture at Old Trafford, we again bossed the encounter and although it did not quite scale the peaks of the glorious 6-1 win there in October, 2011, nobody in a blue shirt was complaining.

Edin Dzeko was the main difference on this occasion although Toure was again at his best, claiming a goal for himself in the final minute to seal United's fate.

The win moved us behind Chelsea in the table as Pellegrini's men began to slowly turn the pressure up and show they had the staying power that eventually took us to the Premier League title.

Dzeko took just 43 seconds to open the scoring and then grabbed his second after the break, just as City were hitting top gear.

After that, only one team was ever going to win the contest and Toure confirmed that late on with a low drive that capped off another wonderful performance.

If you're going to win the title, then a derby double isn't a bad first step.

MANCHESTER CITY: Hart, Zabaleta, Kolarov, Nastasic, Kompany, Fernandinho, Toure, Navas (Milner 69), Nasri, Aguero (Garcia 86), Negredo (Dzeko 75).
Unused: Pantilimon, Lescott, Richards, Jovetic.

MANCHESTER UNITED: De Gea, Evra, Smalling, Vidic, Ferdinand, Carrick, Fellaini, Valencia, Young (Cleverley 51), Welbeck, Rooney. Unused: Amos, Buttner, Kagawa, Nani, Chicarito, Evans.

GOALS: Aguero 17, 47, Toure 45, Nasri 51 (Manchester City); Rooney 87 (Manchester United).

ATTENDANCE: 47,156.

MANCHESTER UNITED 0
MANCHESTER CITY 3
25.03.2014

MANCHESTER UNITED: De Gea, Rafael, Ferdinand, Jones, Evra, Carrick, Cleverley (Kagawa 46), Fellaini (Valencia 66), Mata, Welbeck (Hernandez 77), Rooney. Unused: Lindegaard, Buttner, Fletcher, Young.

MANCHESTER CITY: Hart, Zabaleta, Clichy, Demichelis, Kompany, Fernandinho, Navas (Garcia 68), Toure, Silva, Nasri (Milner 74), Dzeko (Negredo 79). Unused: Pantilimon, Kolarov, Lescott, Jovetic.

GOALS: Dzeko 1, 56, Toure 90.

ATTENDANCE: 75,000.

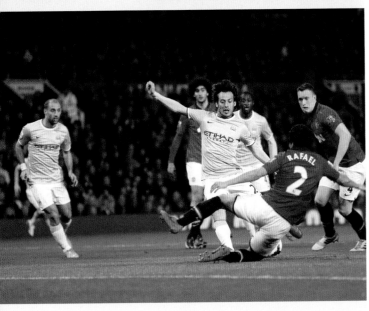

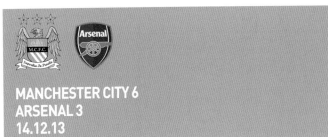

**MANCHESTER CITY 6
ARSENAL 3
14.12.13**

GUNNERS OUTGUNNED

If anybody was still questioning our Premier League title credentials, those queries were silenced on a brilliant day at the Etihad Stadium.

League leaders Arsenal visited Manchester hoping to prove that they could end their title drought but they were comfortably despatched as Pellegrini's men produced a perfect early Christmas present.

Aguero opened the scoring after 14 minutes and although Theo Walcott equalised for Arsene Wenger's men, it then became one-way traffic.

Alvaro Negredo and Fernandinho soon made it 3-1 before Walcott scored his second as he tried desperately to drag the Gunners back into the contest.

However, David Silva, Fernandinho again and Toure all got on the scoresheet to humble the visitors and although Per Mertesacker's late goal did try and add some gloss to the Arsenal scoreline, the message was clear: City are here to stay.

MANCHESTER CITY: Pantilimon, Zabaleta, Clichy, Demichelis, Kompany, Fernandinho, Toure, Nasri (Garcia 90), Silva (Milner 71), Aguero (Navas 49), Negredo. Unused:vHart, Lescott, Dzeko, Kolarov.

ARSENAL: Szczesny, Sagna. Mertesacker. Koscielny (Vermaelen 42), Monreal, Flamini (Gnabry 72), Wilshere, Ozil, Walcott, Ramsey, Giroud (Bendtner 76).
Unused: Fabianski, Rosicky, Arteta, Santi Cazorla.

GOALS: Aguero 13, Negredo 39, Fernandinho 50, 88, Silva 66, Toure 90 pen (Manchester City); Walcott 31, 63, Mertesacker 90 (Arsenal).

ATTENDANCE: 47,329.

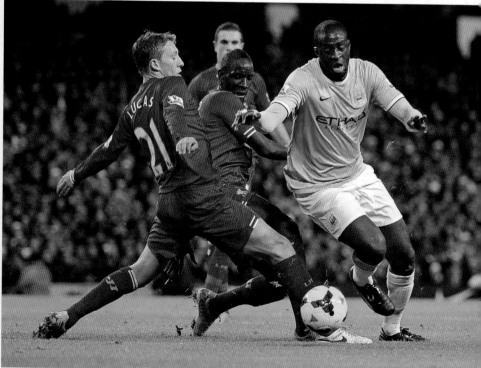

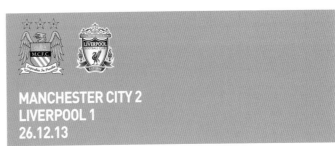

MANCHESTER CITY 2
LIVERPOOL 1
26.12.13

CLOSING IN ON TOP SPOT

If the Arsenal win helped close the gap on the Gunners to three points, this crucial victory heaped even more pressure on the league leaders as it saw us move just a point off the Premier League summit.

If Liverpool had won this match they would have gone top themselves so Premier League clashes rarely come as vital as this one.

Brendan Rodgers's side took the lead at the Etihad courtesy of a strike from Philippe Coutinho but the Blues' inspirational leader Vincent Kompany soon headed us level.

Just before the interval, we then capitalised on poor goalkeeping from Liverpool's Simon Mignolet as he allowed Negredo to chip him and that proved to be enough.

It maintained our flawless home record and meant we had scored in 59 straight home matches in the Premier League.

The Blues were coming to the boil just nicely.

MANCHESTER CITY: Hart, Zabaleta, Kolarov, Lescott, Kompany, Fernandinho, Yaya Toure, Nasri (Milner 72), Silva (Garcia 87), Negredo (Dzeko 77), Navas. Unused: Pantilimon, Clichy, Nastasic, Boyata.

LIVERPOOL: Mignolet, Cissokho, Skrtel, Sakho, Johnson, Lucas (Iago Aspas 82), Allen, Henderson, Sterling, Coutinho (Moses 68), Suarez. Unused: Jones, Kolo Toure, Agger, Alberto, Smith.

GOALS: Kompany 31, Negredo 45 (Manchester City); Coutinho 24 (Liverpool).

ATTENDANCE: 47,351.

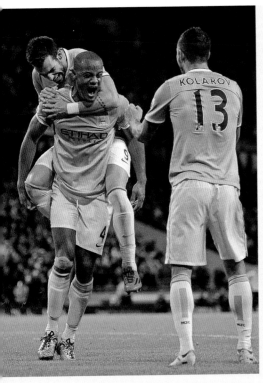

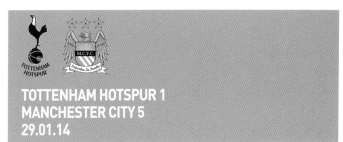

TOTTENHAM HOTSPUR 1
MANCHESTER CITY 5
29.01.14

SPURS BEATEN AGAIN

Tottenham must wonder what they have done to upset the City gods.

Pellegrini's men had hammered Spurs 6-0 at home back in November, and inflicted another heavy defeat in north London.

And they looked simply irresistible as they climbed to the top of the Premier League table.

Sergio Aguero became the fifth-fastest player to 50 Premier League goals as he opened the scoring after 15 minutes before City queued up to get on the scoresheet.

Yaya Toure, Edin Dzeko, Stevan Jovetic and Vincent Kompany all helped pile the misery onto the home side, although Etienne Capoue did grab one back for Spurs.

If City had been slow at getting into top gear this term those worries were now completely abandoned.

We looked sharp, we looked clinical, we looked hungry.

We looked like champions.

TOTTENHAM HOTSPUR: Lloris, Walker, Rose, Dembele (Capoue 46), Dawson, Chiriches, Lennon, Bentaleb, Adebayor, Eriksen (Holtby 83), Sigurdsson, (Naughton 55). Unused: Soldado, Defoe, Chadli, Friedel.

MANCHESTER CITY: Hart, Zabaleta, Kompany, Demichelis, Clichy, Navas, Fernandinho, Toure (Nastasic 69), Silva (Kolarov 80), Aguero (Jovetic 45), Dzeko. Unused: Pantilmon, Lescott, Negredo, Rodwell.

GOALS: Capoue 59 (Tottenham Hotspur); Aguero 15, Toure 51 pen, Dzeko 53, Jovetic 78, Kompany 89.

SENT OFF: Rose 50.

ATTENDANCE: 36,071.

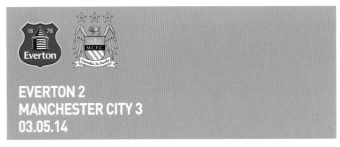

**EVERTON 2
MANCHESTER CITY 3
03.05.14**

COURAGE OF CHAMPIONS

You can teach goalscoring, goalkeeping, defending and attacking.

But you cannot teach nerve or guts or courage.

And City demonstrated all those qualities in abundance at Goodison Park as we returned to the top of the Premier League table from Liverpool on goal difference.

For once, the Stanley Park neighbours were united in wanting an Everton victory but we shrugged off the pressures and got the job done.

Toffees' talent Ross Barkley gave the home side the lead before Aguero equalised to leave the game nicely poised.

However, in the 43rd and 48th minutes, Dzeko proved his worth once again with two fine finishes which helped swing the game in our favour.

Romelu Lukaku scored with 25 minutes left to ensure a nervous ending but we brilliantly battled through and held on for a season-defining three points.

EVERTON: Howard, Coleman, Jagielka (Deulofeu 66), Alcaraz, Baines, Stones, McCarthy, Osman (McGeady 83), Lukaku, Barkley, Naismith. Unused: Robles, Hibbert, Garbutt, Distin, Ledson.

MANCHESTER CITY: Hart, Zabaleta, Clichy, Kompany, Demichelis, Garcia, Toure (Kolarov 66), Milner, Nasri (Silva 74), Dzeko, Aguero (Fernandinho 28). Unused: Pantilimon, Lescott, Negredo, Jovetic.

GOALS: Barkley 11, Lukaku 65 (Everton); Aguero 22, Dzeko 43, 48 (Manchester City).

ATTENDANCE: 39,454.

WINNING IN THE RAIN

Edin Dzeko doesn't let the Manchester rain bother him as his double helped set up a 4-0 win against Aston Villa that put us one game away from the title

MANCHESTER CITY 4
ASTON VILLA 0
07.05.14

VILLA EASED ASIDE

There was no rest for us following the Everton tussle. Another crucial match followed straight away.

And another three points were brilliantly produced, although in a far more relaxing manner.

If the Everton win had demonstrated our willingness to roll our sleeves up, the Villa victory underlined our prolific thirst for goals as this match took us up to 100 Premier League goals for the season.

A goalless first half was a surprise but City were invigorated by the break and Dzeko was at his brilliant best, scoring two goals in eight minutes to send us on our way.

In the last two minutes, Jovetic and then Toure sealed the victory and sent the City fans home happy.

Not as happy as they were a few days later though...

MANCHESTER CITY: Hart, Zabaleta, Kolarov, Kompany, Demichelis, Garcia, Toure, Milner (Jovetic 60), Nasri, Silva (Fernandinho 76) Dzeko (Negredo 86). Unused: Pantilimon, Richards, Lescott, Clichy.

ASTON VILLA: Guzan, Lowton, Vlaar, Baker, Clark (Robinson 79), El Ahmadi, Westwood, Bowery (Bacuna 59), Delph, Bertrand (Grealish 88), Weimann. Unused: Steer, Sylla, Tonev, Holt.

GOALS: Dzeko 64, 72, Jovetic 89, Toure 90.

ATTENDANCE: 47,023.

THE REST OF THE STORY
GAME-BY-GAME

MANCHESTER CITY 4 NEWCASTLE UNITED 0, Etihad Stadium, 19.08.13

"It's a good start but I was confident the team would play well. We worked hard during pre-season, we were trying another style and maybe we must continue to improve but for the first match, it was good"

MANUEL PELLEGRINI

MANCHESTER CITY: Hart, Zabaleta, Clichy, Kompany (Garcia 71), Lescott, Fernandinho, Silva (Negredo 80), Toure, Navas, Aguero (Nasri 62), Dzeko. Unused: Pantilimon, Kolarov, Rodwell, Milner.

NEWCASTLE UNITED: Krul, Debuchy, Yanga-Mbiwa, Coloccini, Taylor, Tiote, Sissoko, Ben Arfa (Sh Ameobi 65), Gouffran (Dummett 45), Cisse, Gutierrez (Anita 44). Unused: Elliot, Marveaux, Sa Ameobi, Obertan.

GOALS: Silva 6, Aguero 22, Toure 50, Nasri 75.
SENT OFF: Taylor 45.
ATTENDANCE: 46,842.

"Corners are the same all around the world. We scored two goals and we had one or two other chances but the game was decided on two corners"

MANUEL PELLEGRINI

CARDIFF CITY: Marshall, Connolly, Taylor, Caulker, Turner, Whitts, Medel, Campbell (Cornelius 90), Kim (Mutch 90), Gunnarsson, Bellamy (Cowie 82). Unused: Lewis, Hudson, Noone, Maynard.

MANCHESTER CITY: Hart, Zabaleta, Garcia, Lescott, Clichy, Toure, Fernandinho (Milner 77), Silva, Navas (Nasri 55), Aguero, Dzeko (Negredo 68). Unused: Pantilimon, Nastasic, Kolarov, Rodwell.

GOALS: Gunnarsson 60, Campbell 79, 88 (Cardiff City); Dzeko 52, Negredo 90 (Manchester City).
ATTENDANCE: 27,068.

MANCHESTER CITY 2 HULL CITY 0, Etihad Stadium, 31.08.13

"It was hard. We know you have to give 100% to win every match but we were more concentrated in defence than the last game against Cardiff"

MANUEL PELLEGRINI

MANCHESTER CITY: Hart, Zabaleta, Kolarov, Nastasic, Lescott, Fernandinho, Toure, Silva (Nasri 65), Aguero (Milner 76), Dzeko (Negredo 46), Navas. Unused: Pantilimon, Clichy, Garcia, Jovetic.

HULL CITY: McGregor, Elmohamady, Figueroa, Chester, Davies, Koren (Boyd 75), Huddlestone, Livermore, Aluko (Quinn 70), Graham, Brady. Unused: Harper, Bruce, Rosenior, Meyler, McShane.

GOALS: Negredo 65, Toure 90.
ATTENDANCE: 46,905.

STOKE CITY 0 MANCHESTER CITY 0, Britannia Stadium, 14.09.13

"It is a good point in a difficult week with all the players we had in the national squad. I am not always happy when I draw but this time it is a good point"

MANUEL PELLEGRINI

STOKE CITY: Begovic, Cameron, Shawcross, Huth, Pieters, Walters, Nzonzi, Adam (Arnautovic 70), Wilson, Etherington (Ireland 70), Jones (Crouch 77). Unused: Sorensen, Whelan, Pennant, Palacios.

MANCHESTER CITY: Hart, Zabaleta, Garcia, Nastasic, Kolarov, Milner, Rodwell, Toure, Nasri (Navas 73), Negredo, Jovetic (Aguero 63). Unused: Pantilimon, Lescott, Dzeko, Fernandinho, Boyata.

ATTENDANCE: 25,062.

ASTON VILLA 3 MANCHESTER CITY 2, Villa Park, 28.09.13

"It is unbelievable we didn't win this match. The team that deserves to doesn't always win"

MANUEL PELLEGRINI

ASTON VILLA: Guzan, Bacuna, Vlaar, Baker, Clark, El Ahmadi, Weimann (Bowery 78), Luna, Delph, Sylla, Kozak. Unused: Steer, Bennett, Helenius, Albrighton, Tonev, Lowton.

MANCHESTER CITY: Hart, Zabaleta, Kolarov, Kompany, Nastasic, Nasri (Navas 65), Fernandinho, Toure, Milner, Negredo, Dzeko (Jovetic 74). Unused: Pantilimon, Richards, Lescott, Clichy, Garcia.

GOALS: El Ahmadi 50, Bacuna 73, Weimann 76 (Aston Villa); Toure 45, Dzeko 56 (Manchester City).
ATTENDANCE: 34,063.

"We needed this victory because we were five points behind Arsenal. We scored three and had four or five more clear chances"

MANUEL PELLEGRINI

MANCHESTER CITY: Hart, Zabaleta, Kolarov (Clichy 58), Lescott, Kompany (Nastasic 35), Fernandinho, Toure, Milner, Silva (Nasri 79), Negredo, Aguero. Unused: Pantilimon, Richards, Clichy, Navas, Dzeko.

EVERTON: Howard, Coleman, Baines, Distin, Jagielka, Naismith, McCarthy, Barkley, Osman (Gibson 63), Mirallas (Deulofeu 63), Lukaku. Unused: Robles, Heitinga, Jelavic, Kone, Stones.

GOALS: Negredo 17, Aguero 45, Howard 69 (og) (Manchester City); Lukaku 16 (Everton).

ATTENDANCE: 47,267.

WEST HAM UNITED 1 MANCHESTER CITY 3, Upton Park, 19.10.13

"We played well, their best player was their goalkeeper. This team should always play in an attacking way because of the players we have"

MANUEL PELLEGRINI

WEST HAM UNITED: Jaaskelainen, Demel (O'Brien 64), Rat, Tomkins, Reid, Noble, Morrison, Diame, Vaz Te (Jarvis 64), Downing, Nolan (Petric 82). Unused: Adrian, Taylor, J.Cole, C.Cole.

MANCHESTER CITY: Hart, Richards, Garcia, Nastasic, Clichy, Fernandinho, Yaya Toure, Nasri (Milner 73), Silva, Aguero (Jovetic 81), Negredo (Kolarov 65). Unused: Pantilimon, Zabaleta, Lescott, Dzeko.

GOALS: Vaz Te 58 (West Ham United); Aguero 16, 50, Silva 79 (Manchester City).
ATTENDANCE: 34,907.

CHELSEA 2 MANCHESTER CITY 1, Stamford Bridge, 27.10.13

"The way we lost the game was incredible. I think Chelsea, Cardiff and Aston Villa did not have chances during the games, but we conceded stupid goals"

MANUEL PELLEGRINI

CHELSEA: Cech, Ivanovic, Cahill, Terry, Cole, Ramires, Lampard (Mikel 65), Hazard (Eto'o 84), Oscar, Schurrle (Willian 65), Torres. Unused: Schwarzer, Azpilicueta, Luiz, Mata.

MANCHESTER CITY: Hart, Zabaleta, Demichelis, Nastasic, Clichy, Garcia (Kolarov 79), Fernandinho, Nasri (Navas 70), Toure, Silva, Aguero (Negredo 86). Unused: Pantilimon, Dzeko, Milner, Richards.

GOALS: Schurrle 33, Torres 90 (Chelsea); Aguero 48 (Manchester City).
ATTENDANCE: 41,495.

MANCHESTER CITY 7 NORWICH CITY 0, Etihad Stadium, 02.11.13

"It was a really good performance. The team played really well during the 90 minutes, and that's very important for me"

MANUEL PELLEGRINI

MANCHESTER CITY: Pantilimon, Zabaleta, Clichy, Nastasic, Demichelis, Fernandinho, Toure, Silva (Navas 73), Nasri (Milner 71), Aguero, Negredo (Dzeko 46). Unused: Hart, Richards, Kolarov, Lescott.

NORWICH CITY: Ruddy, Martin, Olsson, Johnson, Turner, Bassong, Whittaker (Murphy 46), Howson, Hooper (Elmander 46), Fer, Pilkington. Unused: Bunn, Hoolahan, Garrido, Becchio, R Bennett.

GOALS: Johnson 16 (og), Silva 20, Nastasic 24, Negredo 36, Toure 61, Aguero 70, Dzeko 86.
ATTENDANCE: 47,142.

"We will continue the same way because in the four (away) defeats I am sure we are playing the correct way and I hope the wins will come"
MANUEL PELLEGRINI

SUNDERLAND: Mannone, Celustka, Bardsley, Ki, Brown, O'Shea, Johnson (Borini 87), Larsson, Fletcher (Altidore 77) Colback, Giaccherini (Gardner 72). Unused: Cabral, Westwood, Diakité, Mavrias.

MANCHESTER CITY: Pantilimon, Richards (Zabaleta 71), Demichelis, Lescott, Kolarov, Milner, Toure, Garcia (Navas 46), Nasri, Aguero, Negredo (Dzeko 71). Unused: Hart, Clichy, Boyata, Rodwell.

GOAL: Bardsley 21.
ATTENDANCE: 40,137.

"We are working to have one style and continue in the same way. In this style the players are comfortable because they are creative"
MANUEL PELLEGRINI

MANCHESTER CITY: Pantilimon, Clichy, Zabaleta, Demichelis, Nastasic (Lescott 46), Fernandinho, Toure, Nasri (Milner 77), Navas, Negredo, Aguero (Garcia 69). Unused: Hart, Richards, Dzeko, Guidetti.

TOTTENHAM HOTSPUR: Lloris, Walker, Vertonghen, Dawson, Kaboul, Sandro, Paulinho (Dembele 61), Lennon, Holtby (Adebayor 46), Lamela, Soldado (Sigurdsson 61). Unused: Friedel, Chiriches, Townsend, Defoe.

GOALS: Navas 1, 90, Sandro 34 (og), Aguero 41, 50, Negredo 55.
ATTENDANCE: 47,228.

MANCHESTER CITY 3 SWANSEA CITY 0, Etihad Stadium, 01.12.13

"I'm pleased because we won against a difficult team, especially when they had possession. We didn't play well in the first half but in the second we scored two and had more chances"

MANUEL PELLEGRINI

MANCHESTER CITY: Pantilimon, Zabaleta, Lescott, Demichelis, Clichy, Fernandinho, Toure, Navas (Kolarov 76), Nasri, Negredo (Milner 63), Aguero (Dzeko 79). Unused: Hart, Richards, Garcia, Rodwell.

SWANSEA CITY: Tremmel, Tiendalli, Chico Flores, Williams, Davies, Canas, de Guzman, Shelvey, Pozuelo (Dyer 67), Hernandez (Routledge 62), Vazquez. Unused: Vorm, Taylor, Amat, Lamah, Donnelly.

GOALS: Negredo 8, Nasri 58, 77.
ATTENDANCE: 46,559.

WEST BROMWICH ALBION 2 MANCHESTER CITY 3, The Hawthorns 04.12.13

"We played well in the first half and could have scored more. In the last few minutes, maybe all of us were thinking of the next match"

MANUEL PELLEGRINI

WEST BROMWICH ALBION: Myhill, Reid, McAuley, Olsson, Ridgewell, Yacob, Brunt, Amalfitano, Morrison (Vydra 64), Berahino, Long (Anichebe 64). Unused: L Daniels, Gera, Lugano, Popov, Sessegnon.

MANCHESTER CITY: Pantilimon, Zabaleta, Kompany, Demichelis, Kolarov, Fernandinho, Yaya Toure (Rodwell 87), Navas, Nasri (Garcia 75), Aguero (Milner 68), Dzeko. Unused: Hart, Richards, Lescott, Negredo.

GOALS: Pantilimon 85 (og), Anichebe 90 (West Bromwich Albion); Aguero 8, Toure 23, 73 pen (Manchester City).
ATTENDANCE: 22,943.

"It is a good point. I don't feel like we lost two. In all the other games away I felt like we deserved more but here this was the result that both teams deserved"
MANUEL PELLEGRINI

SOUTHAMPTON: Gazzaniga, Chambers, Shaw, Ward-Prowse, Fonte, Lovren, Lallana (Ramirez 85), Cork, Osvaldo (Lambert 77), Davis (Reed 90), Rodriguez. Unused: Yoshida, Hooiveld, Gallagher, Cropper.

MANCHESTER CITY: Pantilimon, Zabaleta, Kompany, Demichelis, Kolarov, Milner (Garcia 62), Toure (Dzeko 79), Fernandinho, Nasri, Aguero, Negredo (Navas 62). Unused: Hart, Lescott, Clichy, Richards.

GOALS: Osvaldo 42 (Southampton); Aguero 10 (Manchester City).
ATTENDANCE: 31,229.

FULHAM 2 MANCHESTER CITY 4, Craven Cottage, 21.12.13

"After slipping back, Navas and Milner made huge contributions. The reaction of the team was very important"
MANUEL PELLEGRINI

FULHAM: Stekelenburg, Riether, Senderos (Amorebieta 37), Hughes, Riise, Dejagah (Kasami 63), Karagounis (Bent 82), Parker, Sidwell, Richardson, Taarabt. Unused: Ruiz, Kacaniklic, Stockdale, Duff.

MANCHESTER CITY: Hart, Clichy, Kompany, Demichelis, Kolarov, Fernandinho, Toure, Nasri (Milner 75), Silva (Garcia 83), Negredo, Dzeko (Navas 57). Unused: Pantilimon, Boyata, Rodwell, Guidetti.

GOALS: Richardson 49, Kompany 68 (og) (Fulham); Toure 23, Kompany 42, Navas 78, Milner 83 (Manchester City).
ATTENDANCE: 25,509.

MANCHESTER CITY 1 CRYSTAL PALACE 0, Etihad Stadium, 28.12.13

"The team that wants to win the title must have different faces. Normally we score lots of goals here but we knew we were not able to do that"

MANUEL PELLEGRINI

MANCHESTER CITY: Hart, Boyata (Negredo 54), Clichy, Nastasic, Kompany, Garcia, Fernandinho (Nasri 54), Silva, Milner (Kolarov 75), Navas, Dzeko. Unused: Pantilimon, Lescott, Rodwell, Toure.

CRYSTAL PALACE: Speroni, Ward, Mariappa, Parr, Gabbidon, Bannan (Gayle 81), Delaney, Puncheon, Jedinak, Bolasie (Williams 76), Jerome (Chamakh 35). Unused: Campana, Phillips, Moxey, Price.

GOAL: Dzeko 67.
ATTENDANCE: 47,250.

SWANSEA CITY 2 MANCHESTER CITY 3, Liberty Stadium, 01.01.14

"It's a very good result. Swansea are a good team at home. Winning the way we won is very important for us"

MANUEL PELLEGRINI

SWANSEA CITY: Tremmel, Rangel, Davies, Canas, Chico, Williams, Hernandez (Lamah 10), de Guzman, Bony, Shelvey (Pozuelo 81), Routledge. Unused: Amat, Taylor, Tiendalli, Alvaro, Zabret.

MANCHESTER CITY: Hart, Zabaleta, Kolarov, Nastasic, Kompany, Fernandinho, Toure, Nasri (Milner 70), Navas (Rodwell 90), Dzeko, Negredo (Garcia 60). Unused: Pantilimon, Lescott, Clichy, Boyata.

GOALS: Bony 45, 90 (Swansea City); Fernandinho 14, Toure 58, Kolarov 66 (Manchester City).
ATTENDANCE: 20,498.

"We didn't have the possession but without the ball we had more goals and chances. In that sense, we are improving, maybe at the start of the season we would have lost"

MANUEL PELLEGRINI

NEWCASTLE UNITED: Krul, Yanga-Mbiwa (Haidara 82), Santon, Williamson, Tiote, Taylor, Sissoko, Anita (Cisse 73), Cabaye, Remy, Gouffran (Ben Arfa 81). Unused: Gosling, Elliot, Marveaux, Sam Ameobi.

MANCHESTER CITY: Hart, Zabaleta, Kolarov, Demichelis, Kompany, Toure (Garcia 60), Fernandinho, Nasri (Milner 76), Silva, Negredo, Dzeko (Navas 51). Unused: Pantilimon, Clichy, Lescott, Richards.

GOALS: Dzeko 8, Negredo 90.
ATTENDANCE: 49,423.

MANCHESTER CITY 4 CARDIFF CITY 2, Etihad Stadium, 18.01.14

"We are playing fantastic football. We play with fantastic intensity and that is how we must continue"

MANUEL PELLEGRINI

MANCHESTER CITY: Hart, Zabaleta, Kolarov, Demichelis, Kompany, Garcia, Toure, Navas (Clichy 82), Silva (Milner 80), Dzeko, Negredo (Aguero 62). Unused: Pantilimon, Nastasic, Lescott, Fernandinho.

CARDIFF CITY: Marshall, Theophile-Catherine, McNaughton (John 68), Caulker, Turner, Noone, Gunnarsson (Eikrem 78), Medel, Mutch, Whittingham (Bellamy 68), Campbell. Unused: Lewis, Kim, Hudson, Odemwingie.

GOALS: Dzeko 14, Navas 33, Yaya Toure 77, Aguero 79 (Manchester City); Noone 29, Campbell 90 (Cardiff City).
ATTENDANCE: 47,213.

MANCHESTER CITY 0 CHELSEA 1, Etihad Stadium, 03.02.14

"We had clear chances to score at least two goals but didn't. It was a very close game to play without Aguero and Fernandinho, but we'll continue and we'll see"

MANUEL PELLEGRINI

MANCHESTER CITY: Hart, Zabaleta, Kolarov, Nastasic, Demichelis, Kompany, Toure, Navas, Silva, Negredo (Jovetic 57), Dzeko. Unused: Pantilimon, Clichy, Boyata, Lopes, Milner, Rodwell.

CHELSEA: Cech, Ivanovic, Azpilicueta, Cahill, Terry, Luiz, Ramires, Matic, Hazard (Ba 90), Willian (Mikel 90), Eto'o (Oscar 83). Unused: Schwarzer, Cole, Lampard, Salah.

GOAL: Ivanovic 32.
ATTENDANCE: 47,364.

NORWICH CITY 0 MANCHESTER CITY 0, Carrow Road, 08.02.14

"We are frustrated because we could not win but we did all we could do. In front of us there was a team that defended well, and we were not very creative"

MANUEL PELLEGRINI

NORWICH CITY: Ruddy, Martin, Yobo, Bassong, Olsson, Redmond, Tettey, Johnson, Pilkington (Whittaker 90), Fer, Hooper (van Wolfswinkel 66). Unused: Bunn, Hoolahan, Garrido, Becchio, Josh Murphy.

MANCHESTER CITY: Hart, Zabaleta, Kompany, Demichelis, Clichy, Navas, Milner, Toure, Silva, Jovetic (Dzeko 61), Negredo (Kolarov 77). Unused: Pantilimon, Richards, Lescott, Rodwell, Lopes.

ATTENDANCE: 26,382.

MANCHESTER CITY 1 STOKE CITY 0, Etihad Stadium, 22.02.14

"It was important to be concentrated for counter-attacks and set-pieces. We controlled the game and it was a matter of time before we scored"
MANUEL PELLEGRINI

MANCHESTER CITY: Hart, Zabaleta, Kompany, Demichelis, Kolarov, Fernandinho (Navas 62), Toure, Nasri, Silva, Dzeko, Negredo (Jovetic 56, (Garcia 68). Unused: Pantilimon, Lescott, Clichy, Milner.

STOKE CITY: Begovic, Pieters, Wilson, Shawcross, Cameron, Arnautovic (Palacios 67), Whelan (Etherington 81), Adam, Odemwingie, Walters (Ireland 77), Crouch. Unused: Sorensen, Muniesa, Wilkinson, Nzonzi.

GOAL: Toure 69
ATTENDANCE: 47,038.

HULL CITY 0 MANCHESTER CITY 2, KC Stadium, 15.03.14

"I trust my players and the team. We kept the ball very well – and without the ball you cannot make damage"
MANUEL PELLEGRINI

HULL CITY: McGregor, Rosenior (Fryatt 79), Elmohamady, Figueroa (Aluko 45), Chester, Davies, Huddlestone, Meyler (Boyd 57), Livermore, Jelavic, Long. Unused: Harper, Bruce, Koren, Sagbo.

MANCHESTER CITY: Hart, Zabaleta, Kompany, Demichelis, Clichy, Garcia, Fernandinho, Toure (Lescott 70), Nasri (Navas 80), Silva (Kolarov 90), Dzeko. Unused: Pantilimon, Milner, Rodwell, Negredo.

GOALS: Silva 13, Dzeko 89.
SENT OFF: Kompany 10.
ATTENDANCE: 24,895.

MANCHESTER CITY 5 FULHAM 0, Etihad Stadium, 22.03.14

"[Yaya Toure] is a very important player and scoring 20 goals for a midfielder is not easy"

MANUEL PELLEGRINI

MANCHESTER CITY: Hart, Zabaleta, Kolarov, Demichelis, Lescott, Fernandinho, Milner, Toure (Navas 68), Nasri (Jovetic 81), Silva (Rodwell 76), Negredo.
Unused: Pantilimon, Clichy, Boyata, Garcia.

FULHAM: Stockdale, Riise, Heitinga, Hangeland, Kvist, Sidwell, Kacaniklic (Roberts 55), Richardson (Holtby 54), Woodrow (Kasami 82), Riether, Amorebieta.
Unused: Stekelenburg, Karagounis, Zverotic, Bent.

GOALS: Toure 26 pen, 54 pen, 65, Fernandinho 84, Demichelis 88.
SENT OFF: Amorebieta 53 (2 yellow cards).
ATTENDANCE: 47,262.

ARSENAL 1 MANCHESTER CITY 1, Emirates Stadium, 29.03.14

"In the first half we played very well but only scored one goal. But they grew after their goal"

MANUEL PELLEGRINI

ARSENAL: Szczesny, Sagna, Mertesacker, Vermaelen, Gibbs, Arteta, Rosicky, Flamini, Cazorla, Podolski (Oxlade-Chamberlain 80), Giroud (Sanogo 84). Unused: Fabianski, Bellerin, Jenkinson, Kallstrom, Gnabry.

MANCHESTER CITY: Hart, Zabaleta, Kompany, Demichelis, Clichy, Fernandinho, Toure, Navas (Milner 63), Silva, Nasri (Garcia 81), Dzeko (Negredo 84). Unused: Pantilimon, Lescott, Kolarov, Jovetic.

GOALS: Flamini 53 (Arsenal); Silva 17 (Manchester City).
ATTENDANCE: 60,000.

"It was important to continue playing the way we did in the second half because I thought it was a great performance"
MANUEL PELLEGRINI

MANCHESTER CITY: Hart, Zabaleta, Kompany, Demichelis, Kolarov, Navas, Fernandinho (Garcia 46), Toure, Nasri, Silva (Jovetic 77), Dzeko (Negredo 65). Unused: Pantilimon, Lescott, Richards, Milner.

SOUTHAMPTON: Gazzaniga, Chambers, Fonte, Lovren, Shaw, Cork (Wanyama 80), Schneiderlin, Davis (Gallagher 85), Lallana, Rodriguez (Ward-Prowse 26), Lambert. Unused: Cropper, Clyne, Guly, Hooiveld.

GOALS: Toure 3 pen, Nasri 45, Dzeko 45, Jovetic 81 (Manchester City); Lambert 37 pen (Southampton).
ATTENDANCE: 47,009.

LIVERPOOL 3 MANCHESTER CITY 2, Anfield, 13.04.13

"We didn't deserve to lose but things happen. We will continue with the same trust until the end of the season"
MANUEL PELLEGRINI

LIVERPOOL: Mignolet, Johnson, Flanagan, Sakho, Skrtel, Gerrard, Henderson, Coutinho (Moses 89), Sterling (Lucas 90), Suarez, Sturridge (Allen 64). Unused: Jones, Toure, Agger, Aspas.

MANCHESTER CITY: Hart, Zabaleta, Kompany, Demichelis, Clichy, Toure (Garcia 18), Fernandinho, Navas (Milner 49), Nasri, Silva, Dzeko (Aguero 67). Unused: Pantilimon, Lescott, Negredo, Kolarov.

GOALS: Sterling 6, Skrtel 26, Coutinho 77 (Liverpool); Silva 57, Johnson 64 (og) (Manchester City).
ATTENDANCE: 44,601.

MANCHESTER CITY 2 SUNDERLAND 2, Etihad Stadium, 16.04.14

"We did not play well but we had in our mind the Liverpool game. We did not deserve to win. We needed a win. We will see what happens but our chances are less"

MANUEL PELLEGRINI

MANCHESTER CITY: Hart, Zabaleta, Kompany, Demichelis, Kolarov, Milner, Garcia, Fernandinho (Rodwell 86), Nasri, Aguero (Jovetic 55), Negredo (Dzeko 67). Unused: Pantilimon, Lescott, Richards, Clichy.

SUNDERLAND: Mannone, Vergini, Alonso, Brown, O'Shea, Cattermole, Colback, Larsson (Giaccherini 67), Johnson, Borini (Scocco 67), Wickham. Unused: Altidore, Ba, Mavrias, Agnew, Ustari.

GOALS: Fernandinho 2, Nasri 88 (Manchester City); Wickham 72, 83 (Sunderland).
ATTENDANCE: 47,046.

MANCHESTER CITY 3 WEST BROMWICH ALBION 1, Etihad Stadium, 21.04.14

"In the second half we tried to keep the result but the team played the way we have the whole year"

MANUEL PELLEGRINI

MANCHESTER CITY: Hart, Zabaleta, Clichy, Demichelis, Kompany, Fernandinho, Garcia, Nasri, Silva (Milner 70), Dzeko (Kolarov 89), Aguero (Jovetic 64). Unused: Pantilimon, Richards, Lescott, Negredo.

WEST BROMWICH ALBION: Foster, Dawson, Jones, Olsson, Ridgewell, Dorrans, Brunt, Amalfitano, Sessegnon (Berahino 76), Vydra (Anichebe 60), Mulumbu (Morrison 84). Unused: Myhill, Reid, Yacob, Lugano.

GOALS: Zabaleta 3, Aguero 10, Demichelis 36 (Manchester City); Dorrans 16 (West Bromwich Albion).
ATTENDANCE: 46,564.

"It was a happy day. Before today we were depending on others. It was important to get a good start but also not to let them score. But it's not finished, we will see who will be the best"

MANUEL PELLEGRINI

CRYSTAL PALACE: Speroni, Mariappa, Dann, Delaney, Ward, Jedinak, Ledley, Bolasie (Ince 73), Puncheon, Chamakh (Gayle 68), Jerome (Murray 68). Unused: Hennessey, Gabbidon, Parr, Dikgacoi.

MANCHESTER CITY: Hart, Zabaleta, Kolarov, Kompany, Demichelis, Garcia, Toure (Fernandinho 66), Milner, Nasri, Dzeko (Negredo 88), Aguero (Jovetic 78). Unused: Pantilimon, Richards, Lescott, Clichy.

GOALS: Dzeko 4, Toure 43.
ATTENDANCE: 24,769.

Manchester City 2013/14
First team fixtures and record

#						F-A	Att	Pos	City scorers and goal times
1	Aug	Mon	19	H	Newcastle United	4-0	46,842	–	Silva 6, Aguero 22, Yaya Toure 50, Nasri 75
2		Sun	25	A	Cardiff City	2-3	27,068	6	Dzeko 52, Negredo 90
3		Sat	31	H	Hull City	2-0	46,903	3	Negredo 65, Yaya Toure 90
4	Sep	Sat	14	A	Stoke City	0-0	25,052	4	–
5		Tue	17	A	Viktoria Plzen (UEFA Champions League)	3-0	11,281	–	Dzeko 48, Yaya Toure 53, Aguero 58
6		Sun	22	H	Manchester United	4-1	47,156	3	Aguero 16, 47, Yaya Toure 45, Nasri 50
7		Tue	24	H	Wigan Athletic (Capital One Cup 3)	5-0	25,519	–	Dzeko 33, Jovetic 60, 83 Yaya Toure 76, Navas 86
8		Sat	28	A	Aston Villa	2-3	34,063	5	Yaya Toure 45, Dzeko 56
9	Oct	Wed	2	H	Bayern Munich (UEFA Champions League)	1-3	45,021	–	Negredo 79
10		Sat	5	H	Everton	3-1	47,267	5	Negredo 17, Aguero 45, Howard og 69
11		Sat	19	A	West Ham United	3-1	34,507	4	Aguero 16, 51, Silva 80
12		Wed	23	A	CSKA Moscow (UEFA Champions League)	2-1	14,000	–	Aguero 34, 42
13		Sun	27	A	Chelsea	1-2	41,495	7	Aguero 49
14		Wed	30	A	Newcastle United (Capital One Cup 4)	2-0	33,846	–	Negredo 99, Dzeko 105 (after extra-time)
15	Nov	Sat	2	H	Norwich City	7-0	47,066	4	Johnson og 16, Silva 20, Martin og 25, Negredo 36, Yaya Toure 60, Aguero 71, Dzeko 86
16		Tue	5	H	CSKA Moscow (UEFA Champions League)	5-2	38,512	–	Aguero pen 3, 20, Negredo 30, 51, 90+2
17		Sun	10	A	Sunderland	0-1	40,137	8	–
18		Sun	24	H	Tottenham Hotspur	6-0	47,227	4	Navas 1, 90+1, Sandro og 34, Aguero 41, 50, Negredo 55
19		Wed	27	H	Viktoria Plzen (UEFA Champions League)	4-2	37,742	–	Aguero pen 33, Nasri 65, Negredo 78, Dzeko 89
20	Dec	Sun	1	H	Swansea City	3-0	46,559	3	Negredo 8, Nasri 58, 77
21		Wed	4	A	West Bromwich Albion	3-2	22,943	3	Aguero 9, Yaya Toure 24, pen 74
22		Sat	7	A	Southampton	1-1	31,229	4	Aguero 10
23		Tue	10	A	Bayern Munich (UEFA Champions League)	3-2	68,000	–	Silva 28, Kolarov pen 59, Milner 62
24		Sat	14	H	Arsenal	6-3	47,229	3	Aguero 14, Negredo 39, Fernandinho 50, 88, Silva 66, Yaya Toure pen 90
25		Tue	17	A	Leicester City (Capital One Cup 5)	3-1	31,319	–	Kolarov 8, Dzeko 41, 53
26		Sat	21	A	Fulham	4-2	25,509	2	Yaya Toure 23, Kompany 43, Jesus Navas 78, Milner 83
27		Thu	26	H	Liverpool	2-1	47,351	2	Kompany 31, Negredo 45+1
28		Sat	28	H	Crystal Palace	1-0	47,107	1	Dzeko 66
29	Jan	Wed	1	A	Swansea City	3-2	20,498	2	Fernandinho 14, Yaya Toure 58, Kolarov 66
30		Sat	4	A	Blackburn Rovers (FA Cup 3)	1-1	18,813	–	Negredo 45
31		Wed	8	H	West Ham United (Capital One Cup SF1)	6-0	30,381	–	Negredo 12, 26, 49, Yaya Toure 40, Dzeko 60, 89
32		Sun	12	A	Newcastle United	2-0	49,423	1	Dzeko 8, Negredo 90+5
33		Wed	15	H	Blackburn Rovers (FA Cup 3 Replay)	5-0	33,102	–	Negredo 45+1, 47, Dzeko 67, 79, Aguero 73
34		Sat	18	H	Cardiff City	4-2	47,213	2	Dzeko 14, Navas 33, Yaya Toure 76, Aguero 79
35		Tue	21	A	West Ham United (Capital One Cup SF2)	3-0	14,390	–	Negredo 3, 59, Aguero 24 (City win 9-0 on aggregate)
36		Sat	25	H	Watford (FA Cup 4)	4-2	46,514	–	Aguero 60, 79, 90+2, Kolarov 87
37		Wed	29	A	Tottenham Hotspur	5-1	36,071	1	Aguero 15, Yaya Toure pen 51, Dzeko 53, Jovetic 78, Kompany 89
38	Feb	Mon	3	H	Chelsea	0-1	47,364	2	–
39		Sat	8	A	Norwich City	0-0	26,832	3	–
40		Sat	15	H	Chelsea (FA Cup 5)	2-0	47,013	–	Jovetic 16, Nasri 67
41		Tue	18	H	Barcelona (UEFA Champions League R16/1)	0-2	46,030	–	–
42		Sat	22	H	Stoke City	1-0	47,038	3	Yaya Toure 70
43	Mar	Sun	2	N	Sunderland (Capital One Cup Final)	3-1	84,697	–	Yaya Toure 55, Nasri 56, Jesus Navas 90 (at Wembley)
44		Sun	9	H	Wigan Athletic (FA Cup 6)	1-2	46,824	–	Nasri 68
45		Wed	12	A	Barcelona (UEFA Champions League R16/2)	1-2	85,957	–	Kompany 89 (Barcelona win 4-1 on aggregate)
46		Sat	15	A	Hull City	2-0	24,895	2	Silva 14, Dzeko 90
47		Sat	22	H	Fulham	5-0	47,262	3	Yaya Toure pen 26, pen 54, 65, Fernandinho 84, Demichelis 88
48		Tue	25	A	Manchester United	3-0	75,203	2	Dzeko 1, 56, Yaya Toure 90
49		Sat	29	A	Arsenal	1-1	60,060	3	Silva 18
50	Apr	Sat	5	H	Southampton	4-1	47,009	3	Yaya Toure pen 3, Nasri 45+1, Dzeko 45+4, Jovetic 81
51		Sun	13	A	Liverpool	2-3	44,601	3	Silva 57, Johnson og 62
52		Wed	16	H	Sunderland	2-2	47,046	3	Fernandinho 2, Nasri 88
53		Mon	21	H	West Bromwich Albion	3-1	46,564	3	Zabaleta 3, Aguero 10, Demichelis 36
54		Sun	27	A	Crystal Palace	2-0	24,769	3	Dzeko 4, Yaya Toure 43
55	May	Sat	3	A	Everton	3-2	39,454	1	Aguero 22, Dzeko 43, 48
56		Wed	7	H	Aston Villa	4-0	47,023	1	Dzeko 64, 72, Jovetic 89, Yaya Toure 90+2
57		Sun	11	H	West Ham United	2-0	47,300	1	Nasri 39, Kompany 49

Manchester City — Player Appearance Grid 2013/14

#	Joe HART	Pablo ZABALETA	Vincent KOMPANY	Joleon LESCOTT	Gael CLICHY	FERNANDINHO	Yaya TOURE	Jesus NAVAS	David SILVA	Edin DZEKO	Sergio AGUERO	Samir NASRI	Javi GARCIA	Alvaro NEGREDO	Costel PANTILIMON	Aleksandar KOLAROV	James MILNER	Jack RODWELL	Matija NASTASIC	Stevan JOVETIC	Dedryck BOYATA	Micah RICHARDS	Marcos LOPES	Richard WRIGHT	Martin DEMICHELIS	John GUIDETTI	Emyr HUWS
1			X			Debut	1	Debut	1 x		1 x	Sub SA62	Sub VK71	Debut DS80	Unused Sub	Unused Sub	Unused Sub	Unused Sub	Unused Sub								
2			X				X		1 x			Sub JN55		Sub ED68 1	Unused Sub	Unused Sub	Sub F77	Unused Sub	Unused Sub								
3				Unused Sub			1			X	X	X	Sub DS66	Sub ED45 1	Unused Sub		Sub SA76		Unused Sub								
4				Unused Sub	Unused Sub			Sub SN73		Unused Sub	Sub SJ62	X		Unused Sub							Debut	X	Unused Sub				
5				Unused Sub	Unused Sub			1 x		Unused Sub	1 x	1		Sub YT80	Sub ED83	Unused Sub	Sub JN67	Unused Sub	Unused Sub								
6				Unused Sub	Unused Sub			1	X	Sub AN75	2 x	1		Sub SA86	Unused Sub		Sub JN71		Unused Sub								
7			X			Sub F45	Sub ML71 1				1 x			Sub ED79	Unused Sub	Unused Sub			Unused Sub	2		Unused Sub	X	Unused Sub			
8				Unused Sub	Unused Sub		1	Sub SN66			1 x	X		Unused Sub	Unused Sub				Unused Sub			Sub ED74	Unused Sub				
9	Unused Sub		Unused Sub					Sub SA70	X	X		Unused Sub		Sub ED57 1	Unused Sub		Sub SN70										
10		X		Sub AK57				Unused Sub		Unused Sub	1 x	Sub SA79		1	Unused Sub	X	Sub VK34		Sub SA82								
11		Unused Sub		Unused Sub			1		Unused Sub		2 x	X	X		Unused Sub	Sub AN66	Sub SN74		Unused Sub		Unused Sub						
12				Unused Sub	Sub SA89		X			Sub AN71	2 x	Sub DS79	X		Unused Sub				Unused Sub		Unused Sub						
13							Sub SN70			Unused Sub	1 x			Sub SA87	Unused Sub	Sub JG79	Unused Sub		Unused Sub						Debut		
14	Unused Sub	Sub MR83			Unused Sub			Sub JR64				Unused Sub		Sub SJ10 1					X		X		X		Unused Sub		
15	Unused Sub		Unused Sub				1	Sub DS73	1 x	X	1	Sub AN45 1		1 x			Unused Sub	Sub SN71			Unused Sub						
16	Unused Sub		Unused Sub		X		Sub SN77		Unused Sub	2	X			3			Sub DS66	Sub F45			Unused Sub						
17	Unused Sub	Sub MR71		Unused Sub			Sub JG45		Sub AN71			X			Unused Sub				Unused Sub	X		Unused Sub					
18	Unused Sub	Sub MN45					2				2 x	X		Sub SA69	Unused Sub		1		Sub SN77	X		Unused Sub					
19		Unused Sub				X	Sub F64	Sub SA46		1	1 x	1 x		Sub SN75 1	Unused Sub		Sub JN76	Sub AN63	Unused Sub								
20	Unused Sub						X			Sub SA79	X	2	Unused Sub	1 x					Unused Sub			Unused Sub					
21	Unused Sub		Unused Sub				2 x				1 x	X		Sub SN77	Unused Sub			Sub SA69	Sub YT88			Unused Sub					
22	Unused Sub		Unused Sub	Unused Sub		X	Sub AN64			Sub YT78	1		Sub JM64	X				X				Unused Sub	X				
23		Sub MR16	Unused Sub						1 x	X	Unused Sub			Sub DS73	Unused Sub	1	1	Sub ED88				Unused Sub	X				
24	Unused Sub		Unused Sub			2	Sub SA50	1 x	Unused Sub	1 x		Sub SN90	1	Unused Sub	Sub DS71										Unused Sub		
25		X					Unused Sub		X	2		Sub DS70		Unused Sub	Unused Sub						Sub PZ12				Unused Sub		Unused Sub
26		1				1	Sub ED58 1		X	X		X	Sub DS84	Unused Sub		Sub SN75 1	Unused Sub				Unused Sub				Unused Sub		
27		1		Unused Sub				Sub AN76	X	1		X	Sub DS86	1 x	Unused Sub		Sub SN71				Unused Sub				Unused Sub		
28			Unused Sub	X	Unused Sub		X			1		Sub F55	Sub DB55	Unused Sub	Sub JM75		1	Sub SN70	Sub JN90		Unused Sub						
29			Unused Sub	Unused Sub	1		X					Sub AN60			Unused Sub		Sub SN70	Sub JN90			■						
30	Unused Sub	Sub DS88	Unused Sub		Unused Sub	X	Sub F64	Sub AN74			1 x			Unused Sub		Sub DS73	Unused Sub				Sub YT66						
31	Unused Sub				Unused Sub	1 x	X	2			3 x		Sub AN79	Unused Sub		Unused Sub					Sub DS73		Sub YT66				
32			Unused Sub	Unused Sub	X		Sub ED52		1 x		1	Sub YT61		Sub SN79	Sub F45				Unused Sub								
33	Unused Sub	Unused Sub		X					2	Sub AN72 1	2 x							Unused Sub			X	Unused Sub	Unused Sub		Debut MR77		
34			Unused Sub	Sub JN82	Unused Sub	1		1 x		1	Sub AN62 1	X		Unused Sub		Sub DS80		Unused Sub							Unused Sub		
35	Unused Sub	Unused Sub		Unused Sub			X		Unused Sub	1 x	X		2	Sub JN79		Sub JG63	Sub SA65										
36	Unused Sub	Sub MR45	Sub JR45	Unused Sub	Unused Sub					3				1	Unused Sub	Sub ML57	X		X	X		Unused Sub					
37		1		Unused Sub		1 x	X	1		X			Unused Sub	Unused Sub	Sub DS80	Unused Sub	Sub YT69	Sub SA45 1				Unused Sub					
38			Unused Sub								X	Unused Sub	Sub AN77	Unused Sub	Unused Sub	Unused Sub	Sub AN57	Unused Sub	Unused Sub								
39			Unused Sub				Sub SJ61				X	Unused Sub	Sub AN77	Unused Sub		Unused Sub	X		Unused Sub	Unused Sub							
40	Unused Sub				Sub DS69	X			Sub SJ61 1	Sub ED80	X	Unused Sub	X				1	X	Unused Sub		■						
41			Sub AK58		X	Sub AN74			Sub JN58	X	Unused Sub	X		Unused Sub		Sub AN56 X		Unused Sub	Unused Sub		■						
42			Unused Sub	Unused Sub	X	Sub F63				Sub SJ68	X	Unused Sub		Unused Sub		Sub AN56 X			Unused Sub								
43	Unused Sub		Unused Sub	Unused Sub		Sub SA58 1	X	X		1	X		Sub DS77	Sub ED88		Unused Sub			Unused Sub								
44	Unused Sub		Unused Sub			X	X	Sub YT53	Sub AN53			X			Unused Sub	Sub JN53	Unused Sub										
45		■	1		Unused Sub		Sub SN75	Sub SA46	X			Unused Sub	Sub DS72	Unused Sub	Unused Sub	Unused Sub			Unused Sub								
46		■	Sub YT71			X	Sub SN81	1 x	X			X	Unused Sub	Sub DS90	Unused Sub	Unused Sub										1	
47			Unused Sub		1	3 x	Sub DS68				X	Unused Sub				Sub YT77	Sub SN82	Unused Sub									
48			Unused Sub		1	X	2 x					Sub JN68	Sub ED79	Unused Sub	Unused Sub	Sub SN74	Unused Sub										
49			Unused Sub									Sub SN81	Sub ED85	Unused Sub	Unused Sub	Sub JN64	Unused Sub										
50			Unused Sub		X	1	X	1 x				Sub F46	Sub ED65	X	Unused Sub	Unused Sub			Sub DS66 1	Unused Sub							
51			Unused Sub	X	X	X			Sub ED68	1	Sub YT19	X	Unused Sub	Unused Sub	Sub JN50												
52			Unused Sub	Unused Sub	1 x			Sub AN69		1	X	Unused Sub	Unused Sub	Sub F87		Sub SA57	Unused Sub					1					
53		1	Unused Sub		X				1 x			Unused Sub	Sub ED89	Sub DS70		Sub SA54	Unused Sub										
54			Unused Sub	Unused Sub	Sub YT66	1 x			1 x			Sub ED88				Sub SA79	Unused Sub										
55			Unused Sub	Sub SA28	Sub SN75				2	1 x		Unused Sub		Sub YT66	Unused Sub		Unused Sub										
56			Unused Sub	Sub DS76	1			X	2 x			Sub ED86	Unused Sub		X	Unused Sub		Sub JM60 1	Unused Sub								
57		1	Unused Sub	Unused Sub	Sub ED69	X	X		1			Sub YT86	Unused Sub		Sub DS76	Unused Sub											

NOTE: Match 25 Only six substitutes named

"THIS SHOWS WE'RE NOT A FLASH IN THE PAN. SAMIR NASRI'S GOAL WAS GREAT AND WE RAN THE CLOCK DOWN. AND I'VE GOT VINCENT KOMPANY'S CAPTAIN'S ARMBAND - I SAW HIM IN THE TUNNEL AND BLAGGED IT OFF HIM!"

NOEL GALLAGHER

"THANK YOU TO ALL THE SUPPORTERS. THEY ARE THE BEST FANS IN ENGLAND. NO MATTER WHERE WE PLAY IT IS ALWAYS FUN." **JAVI GARCIA**

" As a kid, you grow up and
dream of lifting trophies.
I feel like I am living that dream
when I do this. "

– VINCENT KOMPANY, MAY 11, 2014